Endorsements

Virginia has written a beautiful explanation of the Lord's Prayer with simplicity and depth. In these chapters, she shares her heart's desire - that the younger generation may find the meaning and power of sincere prayer, rooted in a personal faith in Christ. Any Christian of any age will be blessed, challenged, and encouraged as they read Guide to Deeper Prayer.

— **Dr. OS and Susie Hawkins**

Dr. OS Hawkins
Senior Advisor and Ambassador at Large for
Southwest Baptist Theological Seminary
and Pastor, Author of the *Code* Series

Susie Hawkins
Author, Speaker

Prayer - We know it's important and we know we should do it. Guide to Deeper Prayer: Digging into the Prayer Jesus Taught *not only explains how to move past "emergency prayers" but explains the relationship side of communicating with your Heavenly Father. It's easy to communicate with someone you have a relationship with, and that relationship grows deeper with communication. The Creator and Sustainer of everything desires a personal relationship with you and He longs to hear your voice. Virginia explains in a straightforward approach with clear application how to develop a strong prayer life. Jesus taught His disciples how to pray; let's learn from His instruction.*

— **Debbie Stuart**
Minister to Women at Green Acres Women;
previously served as Trainer at Lifeway Christian Resources
National Women's Ministry, VP at Hope for the Heart,
Director of Women's Leadership at Women of Faith, and
Women's Ministry Director of Prestonwood Baptist Church

The majesty of God is a thread woven into every page of this book, as is the love of God and His desire to have us live in an abiding love relationship with Him. As Virginia guides us through the prayer Jesus gave us, she helps us realize the depth and expanse of its meaning. This simple prayer, this guide to prayer, leads us to the heart of God and a daily walk with Him in which we can truly experience His joy as our strength.

— **Kaye Johns**
Author, Speaker, Co-founder, and Leader of
PrayerPower Ministries, now known as Tandem Prayer,
Director of Prayer for e3 Partners

GUIDE TO
DEEPER
PRAYER

DIGGING INTO THE
PRAYER JESUS TAUGHT

VIRGINIA GROUNDS

Published by Breakthrough Christian Publishing
BreakthroughChristianPublishing.com

ISBN: 979-8-9907557-6-5 (Paperback)
ISBN: 979-8-9907557-7-2 (ebook)

Library of Congress Control Number: 1-12697895351

Printed in the United States of America.
10 9 8 7 6 5 4 3 2 1

In Memory of

Gene Grounds

Loving husband,
father,
brother,
grandfather, and
great-grandfather,

whose final journal entry is below
exactly as he wrote it:

...rejoice because your names are written in heaven.
...when you pray say: Our Father which are in heaven.
...Hallowed be thy name.
Thy kingdom come,
Thy will be done,
As in heaven, so in earth! ...

Contents

Jesus said,

"Pray then like this:

Our Father in heaven,

Hallowed be your name.

Your kingdom come,

your will be done.

on earth as it is in heaven.

Give us this day our daily bread,

and forgive us our debts,

as we also have forgiven our debtors.

And lead us not into temptation,

but deliver us from evil."

(Matthew 6:9–13)

Dedication

This book is dedicated to our seven grandsons: Tyler, Alex, Bryan, Halen, Preston, Ryan, and Jordan. Your granddaddy and I have loved you all your lives. Before your grandaddy went to heaven, he prayed for each one of you individually by name every day. He loved you so much. My prayer is that this book will speak to you in a way that helps in your spiritual growth and in your prayer life, and that you will teach your children to pray. Even though we have loved you your entire life, God loves you even more. Draw near to him, and he will draw near to you.

Preface

Perhaps you prayed to receive Jesus as your personal Savior as an adult, but what comes next? This book is written for new believers and those who have not yet gone beyond belief to discover all the benefits God has given for you. You will learn how to effectively pray, how to study and apply the Bible, and how to live an abundant life according to God's will and purpose.

I was once where you are. It wasn't until my late twenties that I became a Christian. Of course, all my life I thought I was because I had been taught to be good and my parents dropped me off at church on Sunday mornings. But as I discovered, that is not what made me a Christian. Making a personal commitment by praying to receive Jesus as my personal Savior and believing by faith God rescued me from a life of sin is what made me a Christian. It was Jesus' sacrifice on the cross for me that secured my eternal home with him.

John 3:16 tells us that "God so loved the world that he gave his only Son, that whoever believes in him ... should have eternal life." Therefore, when we call upon the name of Jesus in faith, we are saved by God's grace and not anything we do or have done.

In the culture today, it is more important than ever to know and understand the commitment that is needed for eternal life in heaven. We can't just think we are a Christian going to heaven. We must do something about it with personal confession of our faith in Christ. Then, to enjoy the benefits of our faith, we must live accordingly. How do we know how to live? By studying the Bible and applying biblical principles to our lives. We know as we pray and draw near to God. When we do, he draws near to us. Over time, it becomes a natural part of our day to spend time with the Lord and our lives are transformed to reflect Christ in us.

Old habits are hard to break, but with God's help we can turn from the harmful habits of the past and develop new habits that are beneficial to us, others, and accomplish God's purpose. Dive in to reading this book with a prayer for God to open the eyes of your heart for understanding this new life in Christ you have been given.

Introduction

They laughed. As a new believer, I did not know how to pray. Oh, I knew the rote prayer my parents prayed before a meal. A rote prayer is one memorized and repeated without making it personal from the heart. So, when I was asked to pray at a meal, that is the prayer I said. And they laughed. Not the making fun of me kind of laugh, but the startled laugh that slips out before you can catch it and hold it back.

But it was enough to humiliate me, causing my face to burn. From that moment, I determined to learn to pray God's way. As I searched the Bible, I found the pattern for prayer Jesus taught his disciples. He taught them to make prayer personal in their relationship with God. What I learned is what I am sharing in this book to encourage others in knowing God is our Father in heaven who loves when we communicate with him. And that is what prayer is—simply talking to God. But there are important components to include in our prayers. It is what Jesus taught when he said, "Pray then like this."

But Jesus did not teach this prayer method to unbelievers. It was to those who followed him. Praying without knowing and believing in Jesus is a moot point. It is like sharing your thoughts, needs, and requests with someone you don't know. Then they walk away. Nothing is accomplished. The conversation is not effective.

Prayer with God begins through our personal commitment to receive Jesus as our Savior. It is through him by his Spirit that we can connect with God. Therefore, our prayer begins with acknowledging that God is personal in our lives.

As you read this book, my recommendation is to read one chapter at a time. Think about what the phrase from the Lord's Prayer in each chapter means to you personally. Apply what you learn to your prayer. As you begin a new chapter, repeat the phrase from the previous chapter(s) along with the new phrase added.

My prayer is that we would all be drawn closer to God through a dedicated, consistent prayer life each day.

Chapter One

Our Father

"Our Father"

Nathaniel was two years old, and his upstairs bedroom overlooked his father's workplace. His Momo (that's me) had his attention as she sat in the room with him. But then he heard a noise outside, went to the window, and pulled back the shades. When he saw his father working, Nathaniel redirected his attention only to him, and he began to call to his "Da." He wanted to be where his father was, doing what his father was doing. What was taking place in the room was not as important to him as seeing his father at work.

This is what prayer does for us. It redirects our attention from all else as we call upon our Father in heaven. When we look for God as he works, we should be so interested that we want to join him there.

In Matthew 6:9, Jesus invited his disciples to intimacy with God. The prayer begins like the greeting in a letter addressing who we are speaking to. When Jesus began with, "Our Father," he was telling the disciples that not only was God his Father, but also their Father.

How Is God Our Father?

When a child comes into a family, whether by birth or adoption, the father beams with love as he holds his child for the first time. The look on a young father's face as he investigates the face of his child is the sweetest I have ever seen. As believers, God is our Father because he adopted us into his family the moment we received Jesus as our Lord and Savior. He loves us more than any earthly father could. In that moment of our commitment to him, which Jesus described as being born again, it is easy to imagine how sweet the love of God is for us. We are to love him as an innocent child. He is our Father because he created us for a relationship with him. As the apostle Paul wrote:

> *But when the fullness of time had come,*
> *God sent forth his Son, born of woman, born*
> *under the law, to redeem those who were under*
> *the law, so that we might receive adoption as*
> *sons.*
>
> *And because you are sons, God has sent the*
> *Spirit of his Son into our hearts, crying "Abba!*
> *Father!" (Galatians 4:4–6 ESV)*

Understanding who God is helps us to be content with who he created us to be. We can gain acceptance of our life circumstances as we know more about his attributes and character. This gives us a deeper level of trust and peace in his answers to our prayers.

But we must have a correct concept of God to move forward in our faith and grow spiritually.

Author A.W. Tozer wrote, "A right concept of God is basic, not only to systematic theology but to practical Christian living as well. What comes to mind when we think about God is the most important thing about us."[1] And the apostle Paul wrote:

> *For his invisible attributes, namely, his eternal*
> *power and divine nature, have been clearly*
> *perceived, ever since the creation of the world,*
> *in the things that have been made. So, they are*
> *without excuse. (Romans 1:20 ESV)*

This verse in Romans tells us the entire world bears witness to God through its beauty, productivity, and purpose.

Therefore, those who do not believe have no excuse for their unbelief as they look around and see all God's work in creation. God is our creator.

"A right concept of God is basic, not only to systematic theology but to practical Christian living as well. What comes to mind when we think about God is the most important thing about us."

Yet, even we as believers fail at times to appreciate and acknowledge everything God created to sustain us and made possible for us to enjoy. We are without excuse as we reject the Word of God and his work by thinking we can do what we want without consequences.

This is why it is so important to know *who* God is and *how* he is in attribute and character.

How Is God Different?

There are attributes of God that belong to him only. They are not shared with us on earth. Why? Because if we had those attributes, we would tend to believe we don't need God. Understanding what these are should cause us to be in awe of our heavenly Father. They give us reason to worship and praise our Father. That is how our prayers should begin. This is what Jesus is teaching when he said, "Our Father," because there is no one like him. We find revelation about who God is throughout the Bible. He is called by many names. We will learn about these as we go along.

But first, what is the difference between an attribute and a characteristic? God's incommunicable, divine attributes cannot be communicated by humanity. That means we cannot pass them on to others because we don't possess them. They originated with God, and they are God's, unique to his nature. A characteristic, on the other hand, is a feature or quality serving to identify. The traits of goodness, mercy, kindness, love, patience, faithfulness, and more are accessible to us as the fruit of his Spirit. These are character traits God shares with us to develop Christlike behavior in us. As we are transformed more and more into the image of God, we exhibit these characteristics to others. For example, we can give love. We can show mercy.

God's characteristics can be ours; his attributes cannot. In thinking about toddlers, they always seem to want what another child has. If the other child does not share, there may be crying, screaming, pouting, or hurt feelings even when they have something better in their hands. If we cry and pout over what we feel we deserve from God, and he doesn't give it, we are like those toddlers in God's eyes. When in that state, we miss what is right in front of us in what he has given us. We miss the importance of why God's divine attributes are not ours.

Psalm 139 is a passage of Scripture best known for its revelation of when life begins. But if we look at this chapter only from that perspective, we miss the attributes of God found in the passage. In the first few verses, we see God knows us: "O Lord, you have searched me and known me!" (Psalm 139:1).

God knows everything about everything. The word for describing this attribute of God is *omniscient. Omni* means "all" and *scient* means "knowing." God is all-knowing—all-knowledge. He knows everything about us, and everything going on in our nation and the world today.

A real-life example of God's knowledge of us is reflected in how this book came to be. The Lord put this book idea in my heart because of a conversation I had with Ryan, our grandson. It had only been three days since my husband went to heaven. God knew what Gene's last journal entry was, but I did not. I didn't find it until the book was half-written (see memorial page). Therefore, this writing is God's plan, not mine. It is committed to his work for his glory and the benefit of others. Then, four months later, at my sister-in-law's gravesite, the pastor asked everyone to recite the Lord's Prayer. God, who knows everything, knew he would place Jesus' pattern for prayer before me three times during the writing of the book.

When we understand that he knows everything, it helps us to trust him with *everything*. He knows it all, and his purpose will not be thwarted (Job 42:2; John 16:30). The Old Testament is filled with descriptions of God's thoughts about the behavior of humanity. He knows the priorities of the heart and responds accordingly to lead us to what is best for us. From his all-knowing, he knew our need for a Savior and began the process of preparing a way for unity with him through Jesus. His knowledge is infinite—without limit. God is not limited in what he knows because he knows it all. His knowledge is of any time, past, present, and future. Out of his knowledge comes wisdom which he gives to us according to what we can emotionally and spiritually handle.

Out of his knowledge, he determines the importance of our actions as he makes decisions for guiding us in the right direction. He numbers our steps, searches our hearts, and minds, and knows our thoughts and words before we say them. I find this fascinating that he knows my words before I speak them. But it makes sense when you think about his Spirit through Christ living within us. Because he knows our thoughts, and our thoughts become words, therefore, he knows what we will say before we speak. Knowing this should help us to ask each day for God to hold our thoughts captive to the obedience of Christ. This is a phrase from 2 Corinthians 10:5 talking about destroying the strongholds of spiritual warfare by thinking thoughts that line up with the life of Christ and his words. I have prayed this prayer many times throughout my spiritual growth to help me keep my mouth shut rather than reacting in a negative way. It takes time for this habit to take hold, but prayer helps the practice.

His perfect knowledge gives us security for the future. He is the only one who was able to redeem us from this sinful world. He makes a way when there seems to be no way. He knows us so well and knows our needs even before we ask because he is omniscient—our all-knowing God. Because he knows us so well, he does not share all his knowledge with us. He knows our minds could not contain it. It is for our protection that we do not know all God knows.

If you are a multi-tasker, and I am, our minds are filled with multiple activities and details to be taken care of each day. When we overcommit or a crisis occurs, the pressure on our mind is severe. This is called stress and feels like extreme pressure squeezing the head. Eventually we begin to shut down and are not able to accomplish anything. This is why God does not share all his knowledge with us. He knows what we can handle and what we cannot. But he does give the wisdom we need to know for life and godliness. As the psalmist wrote, "You make known to me the path of life; in your presence there is fullness of joy; at your right hand are pleasures forevermore" (Psalm 16:11). There is joy in the presence of the Lord, and the path of life is our covenant relationship with him to enjoy his presence.

When the psalmist said, "Such knowledge is too wonderful for me; it is high; I cannot attain it" (Psalm 139:6), he is acknowledging God's knowledge as something he cannot achieve. The secret wonder of it can never be reached.

God is our Father in heaven. As Nathaniel's father on earth was at work, he knew what he was doing in his work. He had the knowledge to do the job. But Nathaniel did not have the knowledge to do what his father was doing. He just wanted to be with him. It brought him joy to be in the presence of his father. He was fascinated by watching him at work and experienced the love of Tyler, his father.

This picture is beautiful to me. When we think about God as our all-knowing heavenly Father extending his love to us, our hearts should be filled with that same desire: to watch him at work wanting to do our part to expand the kingdom of God even when we don't know everything.

And so, we pray in this way... *Our Father, I want to know more about you. Help me to grow in my faith. I worship you, oh Lord, for your wisdom and knowledge—the wisdom to guide me with the knowledge you teach me. And because you know everything about me, I ask for the understanding to be faithful to you and your Word. Amen.*

Chapter Two

God Is Everywhere

"Our Father, in heaven"

Everywhere I am, God is there. God is *omnipresent*—he is all-present everywhere at the same time. This attribute describes his relationship to time and space. He transcends the limitations of space as he is with us every moment. How is this possible? By his Spirit sent from above. The Spirit of the living God has written his presence on our hearts with the blood of Christ. This is how he knows all about us. This is how he is everywhere. He is Emmanuel, God with us. As David wrote in his psalm:

> *Where shall I go from your Spirit?*
> *Or where shall I flee from your presence?*
> *If I ascend to heaven, you are there!*
> *If I make my bed in Sheol, you are there!*
> *If I take the wings of the morning and dwell in*
> *the uttermost parts of the sea,*
> *even there your hand shall lead me,*
> *and your right hand shall hold me.*
> *(Psalm 139:7–10 ESV)*

David knew he was not worthy to be in the presence of God. He knew his human nature wanted to do right according to his own will and desire, not God's. He wanted to flee from having his activities visible to God. But he also knew God's omnipresence would not allow that. David referred to the supernatural spirit as one he cannot get away from even at the break of dawn and to the remote parts of the sea.

We were on a cruise once that went to an island in the middle of the ocean. On our way, all we could see was water. It was a daunting sight to realize we were in the middle of nowhere with no land in sight. But according to the words of the psalmist, God was right there with us, even though it seemed we were all alone.

There may be times when you feel all alone in a sea of doubt, fear, or hopelessness, distant from God and everyone else. Knowing the ever-presence of God should bring us comfort and hope for tomorrow. Prayer helps. It has helped me more times than I can count. Through prayer, trust in God is strengthened in a way that holds us up in a time of loss. There is no other explanation for the peace I experienced through my husband's illness and death. Jesus was my anchor and resting place, with me all the time. We can't run from him or hide from him, so why not embrace faith in him to see us through every circumstance of life.

The prophet Jeremiah also understood this when he wrote:

> *Can a man hide himself in secret places.*
> *So, I cannot see him? declares the Lord.*
> *Do I not fill heaven and earth? declares the*
> *Lord. (Jeremiah 23:24 ESV)*

He knows you, he is with you, and he sees you. You are never alone without his wisdom to guide you, his presence to comfort you, and his vision like an x-ray to know your needs.

Therefore, as you pray, thank the Lord for these things.

> *Heavenly Father, thank you for your presence*
> *and assurance that I am never alone. Thank you*
> *for knowing my needs even before I ask because*
> *you see me. I am not invisible to you. Help me*
> *to recognize your guidance so I don't have the*
> *desire to run in a different direction. You are*
> *amazing, Lord. Amen.*

Up to this point, we have explored the importance of beginning your prayer with praise, acknowledging God's knowledge and presence. Now we look at another of God's attributes to be thankful for: he is all-powerful.

Power belongs to God. The word for this attribute is *omnipotent.* *Potent* means mighty, powerful. God has unlimited power to bring to existence or cause to happen whatever he wills for whoever he chooses. The psalmist reminds us, "Once God has spoken; twice I have heard this; that power belongs to God" (Psalm 62:11). God is all-powerful. When we acknowledge he is all-knowing and all-powerful, we can trust his power to work in everything he knows about us, including our difficulties. It was by God's powerful use of the cross that we are saved for eternity with him. The apostle Paul tells us:

> For the word of the cross
> is folly to those who are perishing,
> but to us who are being saved
> it is the power of God.
> (I Corinthians 1:18)

The idea of the word "perishing" is ruin or loss. It is a metaphor of the spiritual destitution of those who do not have faith in Christ. Folly in this verse is the same as foolishness. Those who don't believe think those of us who do are foolish. They think believing in Jesus for eternal life is foolish. But in the same sentence, the explanation is clear. They are perishing. Eternal life in heaven will not exist for them unless they believe in Jesus as the Savior of the world, that he is God's Son sent to earth to die for us on the cross so we can be set free from sin and death.

Is faith in Christ folly to you? I hope not. If you are unsure, you can pray to believe and receive Jesus as your personal Savior. The apostle Paul tells us in Romans 10:9, "If you confess with your mouth that Jesus is Lord and believe in your heart that God raised him from the dead, you will be saved." To be saved means to be made whole. Do you feel there is something missing in your life, like there is a hole in your heart? That place is reserved for Jesus. Fill it with his grace by faith. Our all-powerful God can fill our heart with the peace of Christ no matter what we have done in the past.

There was a woman who was considered unclean due to her lifestyle. It was said she had been with many men. When she learned Jesus was eating at the home of a community leader, she brought an alabaster flask of ointment. This compares to the most expensive perfume of today. As she stood behind Jesus, she wept. I imagine she wept for the hopelessness she felt, the life she lived, but dared to believe Jesus could help her. With her tears and costly perfume, she washed his feet using her hair as a towel. Then she did something unimaginable. She kissed his feet. The Pharisees were appalled that Jesus did not send her away. Instead, he forgave her.

> *And he said to her, "Your sins are forgiven."*
> *... And he said to the woman, "Your faith has*
> *saved you; go in peace." (Luke 7:48, 50)*

What stands out to me from this story is she approached Jesus but stood behind him. She cried for want of what he could give but didn't feel worthy because of her past. But Jesus knew exactly who she was and what she had done. He not only accepted her and forgave her, but by doing so, he made her feel worthy, probably for the first time in her life. Jesus has the power to forgive and fill the empty places of the heart, making us whole. He gives supernatural power, but we cannot give it to others. We cannot make anyone whole or give the kind of forgiveness that grants eternal life.

I can certainly relate to this woman, as probably many can. Someone who never felt worthy or loved, with a past I'm not proud of, until the love of my life and his family pointed me to Jesus who loved me first. Faith in Jesus filled the hole in my heart, and he can do the same for you by his power. It is a power we don't have because it is supernatural. Faith is a moral conviction of the truthfulness of God, especially reliance upon Christ for salvation, believing in something we cannot see. But God is real. And he loves you with an everlasting love no matter who you are or what you have done.

Referring back to 1 Corinthians 1:18, the Pharisee in the story about the woman is an example of what it looks like to think you believe when you sit in judgment of others, thinking they are foolish. "Now when the Pharisee who had invited him saw this, he said to himself, 'If this man were a prophet, he would have known who and what sort of woman this is who is touching him, for she is a sinner'" (Luke 7:39). Notice the Pharisee was thinking to himself. Yet, Jesus knew what he was thinking. Our all-knowing God knows our thoughts.

This same power of God is perfected in our weakness. The woman in this story was weak, weary, and desperate for a touch from Jesus. The treasure of Jesus in our humanity, metaphorically of the heart, shows that surpassing power belongs to God and not to us. Surpassing power means to "throw beyond, exceeding greatness." He takes us beyond our weakness to a strength that can only come from him, and that is praiseworthy!

God's power trumps the occult. In Acts 19:11–20, the apostle Paul was preaching in Corinth, and his message was rejected. He left and passed through Ephesus where he met some disciples. He took them with him to Asia where evil practices of the occult were taking place. But God did extraordinary miracles by Paul's hands and the evil spirits came out of them. Paul may have had that situation in mind when he encouraged the Ephesian believers to remember that regardless of what they faced, God's power was stronger (Ephesians 3:20–21). He was making clear to them that the power of God trumps all else so they would not fall into the trap of the occult.

There was a time I read passages of Scripture like this and thought, that was then, this is now. I never thought to see in our day the trappings of the occult taking place in our nation. Evil is rampant. When we see these atrocities going on around us, it would be easy to give up on God. But when you begin to pray and understand the Bible, you realize that what is foretold in God's Word is being played out right now. Rather than despair, this should give us hope. Because we know how the story ends. God wins! His power is greater. Nevertheless, we need revival in this land. Revival begins in our hearts.

There is a phrase in the Ephesians passage that says "according to" God's power at work within us. That phrase indicates the free will he has given us in how much of his power we are willing to receive. As we open our hearts and minds to receive what God gives, we can overcome anything because his power is at work within us. There is no power greater than God's. We need to understand it is this that keeps the world on its axis. He controls the sun, moon, stars, and yes, even the weather.

My great-grandson lives in an area that is warm all year. But a couple of years ago, a cold front blew in. The weatherman predicted snow even though that was unusual for the area. Nathaniel was so excited. The next morning, he ran to the window, and—no snow. In a dejected voice he said, "No snow. I guess God made a mistake." I was standing there and heard him. I said, "No, honey, God doesn't make mistakes. But sometimes people can misunderstand and make a mistake in what they say."

God has the power to control the weather. And even when we predict something is going to happen, that doesn't mean it will.

Our God is sovereign. He controls everything. But just as his knowledge is too much for our minds, all his power is more than our bodies can withstand. He alone possesses power that finds its existence in himself. It is the power of his Spirit which gives us strength.

What have we learned?

- In God's omniscience, he saw our need for a Savior.
- In his omnipresence, he sent Jesus to meet our need for relationship with God.
- In his omnipotence, he equipped us with strength, and made deliverance possible for us to be with him forever.
- From these three attributes, God meets the needs of our mind, spirit, and body. He is our everything.

So, why do we need to know these things as it relates to the Lord's Prayer?

- It is so we know how and what to praise him for.
- It gives us assurance of how much God loves us.
- We learn to trust him because of who he is.
- We learn to walk in his ways as he leads us.
- We learn to worship God our creator and heavenly Father for who he is and all he has done for us.

Therefore, we pray:

> *Lord, as I come into your presence, I worship you for your great and mighty deeds. Because you know my needs before I ask, I worship you. I am so thankful for your presence with me always and your power that works to bring deliverance for those who believe. It is to you and you alone that I give my praise. Thank you for blessing me. Amen.*

Guide to Deeper Prayer

Chapter Three

God Does Not Change

"Our Father, in heaven"

Have you ever seen someone after you've been apart for years, yet they said you haven't changed a bit? It sounds good. We would like to believe it. Then we look in the mirror. We appreciate the compliment, but we know we have changed both on the inside and the outside.

In an ever-changing world, God does not change. This attribute of God is his immutability. God is immutable. He is the same yesterday, today, and forever. What we learn about him from Scripture is the same today as it was in the Bible. His love for us will never change. His plan of salvation will not change. His wisdom is always the same. He does not change, but we as humans do, and more so as we grow in our faith day by day. It is God's plan for us to be transformed into who he created us to be. Yet we can count on him for stability because the same promises he made in the days of the Bible are still promises for today. The God who created Adam is still the same God who created us in our mother's womb. He is immutable.

God Is Incomprehensible – We will never be able to fully understand everything about God. There are things about him that don't make sense to us. We ask why he allows some things and not others. But we may never have an answer. This is where faith and trust come in. We trust that because he knows all, is with us everywhere, has the power to do something about circumstances, and does not change, we can rest knowing he is working for our good.

We get a glimpse of what this looks like from the story of Moses and the children of Israel in Egypt (see the book of Exodus). God sent ten plagues on Egypt that were hard to understand, but in reading the whole story, we discover the purpose was to deliver the Hebrew people from bondage in Egypt.

An answer then to why God allows some things is *deliverance*. How and when, we do not know, but deliverance comes. From his Word, we know believers will be delivered from an evil world when Jesus comes to claim his church. With the increase of lawlessness, violence, and false prophets today, it could be any time. That is a reason it is so important to make prayer a priority in our lives. Prayer keeps us near to God. He is our hedge of protection as the world is going crazy. Jesus has overcome the world. In his words:

> *I have said these things to you,*
> *that in me you may have peace.*
> *In the world you will have tribulation.*
> *But take heart; I have overcome the world.*
> *(John 16:33)*

The incomprehensible, unchanging power of God is greatly displayed in Jesus from his virgin birth to the resurrection from the grave and ascension to the Father. How can we not put our faith and trust in him?

There are so many other attributes of God, too many to list. But the Bible is filled with them. You can do a search for attributes of God on the internet, or a Bible app. Why aren't all his attributes made available to us? Because to do so would tempt us to use them in getting our way when it is not best for us. And to do so would tempt us to use that same power for ungodly purposes. But knowing these things about him gives us cause to worship our holy God.

What does it mean to pray to our Father?

The psalmist gives us an idea of what it means to pray to our Father in heaven. His words are a call to worship.

> *O come, let us worship and bow down;*
> *let us kneel before the LORD our Maker!*
> *For he is our God.*
> *(Psalm 95:6–7a)*

In fact, this psalm is not only a call to worship, but an example of how to worship. The list in verses 1–7 include:
- Singing, making a joyful noise
- Being thankful in God's presence
- Acknowledging his greatness and sovereignty
- Acknowledging his creation
- And understanding that he possesses all of it.

It tells us to acknowledge God for who he is and the great things he has done. It means to stand in awe and worship through praise for his attributes. When we open our prayer with worship and praise, we are humbling ourselves in acknowledgment of who he is and directing our attention to him alone. Praise prepares our hearts to hear a word from God our Father.

To put it in perspective, when you call someone you cannot see, but you know they are nearby, don't you call them by name? The same is true of prayer. You begin by calling God by name—Father. By addressing God as Father, what we're doing is identifying as his child and coming to him on that basis. (See Matthew 7:9–11.) He will not turn us away.

We identify with him by acknowledging his character and saying what is in our hearts. It might look something like this:

> *Father, you know all about me and I trust your purpose for me will never change because you never change. Thank you for your power at work within me and your presence with me all the time, no matter where I go. Amen.*

Then you move into the next part of Jesus' prayer from Matthew 6, "in heaven."

Chapter Four

Who Is in Heaven

"Our Father, in heaven"

My husband's personality was such that he was curious about everything and had to know what was going to happen before it happened. I used the acronym FOMO before it became a well-known phrase: the fear of missing out. Who said what? How was work? When were the boys coming to see us and what they would do? What were we doing for the summer? Who was I talking to and what did we talk about? For vacations or other trips, what were we going to do, where were we going, what would we see, who was going to be there? After a few years of marriage, I realized it was not nosiness, but the curious nature he was born with. His mother said he was always a curious child.

He was in hospice nine months before he went to be with Jesus. During that time, he read everything he could get his hands on about heaven. He wanted to know all he could know about it before he arrived there. In another journal, I found Scripture after Scripture he had written about heaven. Of course, it would be impossible to know everything about heaven, and I am sure he was awestruck when he saw the place of his eternity. I am sure it was so far above his imagination or what he had read that he fell on his face at Jesus' feet, humbled and astonished at what was before him.

But there is one thing we can be sure of. God is there. He is our Father who is in heaven. Jesus sits at his right hand, and we bow before him casting our crowns at his feet. The crowns are the rewards we receive in heaven for what we have done. The Bible tells us this is so. Jesus said it was so when he taught the disciples how to pray "Our Father in heaven."

The description we have of the new heaven is listed in Revelation. It is a beautiful place with mansions waiting for us. Heaven is real. When we acknowledge God is our Father and we worship him, we also acknowledge he is in heaven and praise him for preparing a place for us. Heaven is a mansion beyond anything we could build or imagine on this earth.

What we learn about heaven from the Bible is amazing.

1. **There Is Rejoicing in Heaven**

God rejoices in heaven when someone on earth turns away from the activities of the world and turns their attention to him. This is called repentance. Jesus tells the story of one lost sheep out of one hundred. The shepherd left the ninety-nine in search of the one. When the lost sheep is found, he carries it back where it belongs, with him. He rejoices over the one who was lost but now is found.

> *Rejoice with me, for I have found my sheep that*
> *was lost. Just so, I tell you, there will be more*
> *joy in heaven over one sinner who repents than*
> *over ninety-nine righteous persons who need no*
> *repentance. (Luke 15:6–7)*

To repent is to change direction and go the other way. It is to turn from sin (the ways of the world) and turn to the righteousness of God through Christ Jesus. Jesus is not saying heaven doesn't rejoice over the righteous, rather those who believe they are righteous and think they need not repent. We saw a visual of this in the movie *Jesus Revolution*. Many church members were dispassionate about the work of God. They sat stoic and judgmental in their pews while people off the street were repenting and receiving Jesus as their Savior. The members wanted no part of them, but heaven was rejoicing over the lost who had been found.

Are you feeling lost today, that no one cares? You can know Jesus cares. He is searching for you. Even though he knows where you are, he is waiting for you to allow yourself to be found. There he will welcome you with open arms and place you where you belong.

2. **All Authority Comes from Heaven**

When Jesus came to earth and began teaching around the age of thirty, he was given all authority by his Father in heaven. His authority held the same power of God and revealed the deity of Christ—that he was God from heaven in human form.

After Jesus rose from the dead, he revealed himself to his disciples. When they saw him, they worshiped him, but some doubted it was him. So, Jesus said to them, "All authority in heaven and on earth has been given to me. Go therefore and make disciples of all nations, baptizing them in the name of the Father and of the Son and of the Holy Spirit" (Matthew 28:18–19).

God gave authority to Jesus in heaven and earth. Jesus passed authority to those who follow him to make disciples by teaching them and baptizing them in the name of the Holy Trinity—Father, Son, Spirit—equal in deity with different roles.

3. **Treasure in Heaven**

Believers will receive rewards in heaven, crowns to cast at the feet of Jesus. He is our treasure. In Luke 18:22, Jesus said those who follow him will have treasure in heaven. Our relationship with him is our gateway. He is the way, truth, and life. No one gets to the Father but through him. This is so important to grasp. There are those who believe there are many ways to heaven, and everyone goes. This is a false belief. Jesus is the only way. No one goes to heaven except through a relationship with him.

The Bible tells us to call upon the name of Jesus and you will be saved, meaning you will have eternal life. "For everyone who calls on the name of the Lord will be saved" (Romans 10:13).

"So, faith comes from hearing, and hearing through the word of Christ" (Romans 10:17). Jesus spoke and taught about faith. It is his name to call for eternal life. He is the only way. No one else hung on a cross, shedding blood to atone for the sin of us all.

4. **Citizenship in Heaven**

A place of birth or nationality of parents is what makes you a citizen of a nation. However, by naturalization, a person can also be given rights and responsibilities of citizenship. The good qualities of a citizen are truth, justice, and equality. Respect for others is added to the list.

In our humanity, we are born on earth. We are to respect the place of our citizenship. But there is a second birth: our spiritual birth. Once we receive Jesus as Savior, we are born into the spiritual realm with citizenship in heaven secured by the Holy Spirit as a guarantee. Therefore, our response to our heavenly citizenship while on this earth is to live as good citizens with truth, justice, and equality. With the help of the Holy Spirit, we can do so in preparation for heaven.

In our present society, we can see Philippians 3:17–4:1 lived out before our eyes.

> *Brothers, join in imitating me, and keep your*
> *eyes on those who walk according to the example*
> *you have in us. For many, of whom I have*
> *often told you and now tell you even with*

*tears, walk as enemies of the cross of Christ.
Their end is destruction, their god is their belly,
and they glory in their shame, with minds
set on earthly things. <u>But our citizenship is
in heaven</u> [emphasis added], and from it we
await a Savior, the Lord Jesus Christ, who will
transform our lowly body to be like his glorious
body, by the power that enables him even to
subject all things to himself. Therefore, my
brothers, whom I love and long for, my joy and
crown, <u>stand firm thus in the Lord</u> [emphasis
added], my beloved.*

In Philippians, Paul is addressing the believers in
Philippi, encouraging them to stand firm in their faith
when enemies of the cross seek to destroy everything
they stand for. He describes those enemies in this way:

- They are unbelievers, mockers, and persecutors of
the faith.
- They are destructive. Look around the nation today.
We are seeing destruction such as we have never seen
before with no accountability or consequence.
- Their god is their belly. In other words, their goal is
to satisfy their desires for ungodly things.
- They are not embarrassed by the shameful things they
do. In fact, are blatant about it, exposing it for all to
see and indoctrinating children by their behaviors.

- They only think about the here and now, setting their minds on what they can get and do today with no thought to the future or who they harm.

We know these things are happening, but we do not lose hope in the promise of a better place—heaven is our eternal home. Therefore, we are to behave worthy to be citizens of heaven.

5. **Hope of Inheritance in Heaven**

   When we say, "Our Father in heaven," we acknowledge his authority over us. He created us. He rejoices over us; he guides us with his authority. We are his treasure; he is our salvation—our treasure in heaven. Heaven is our true home. We are citizens there, just passing through this place on our way home. It is through Jesus we enter heaven. He is the way, truth, and life. As if this were not enough to bless us, the apostle Peter also assured us of an inheritance in heaven:

   > *Blessed be the God and Father of our Lord Jesus Christ! According to his great mercy, he has caused us to be born again to a living hope through the resurrection of Jesus Christ from the dead to an inheritance that is imperishable, undefiled, and unfading. (I Peter 1:3–4)*

- **Our inheritance in heaven will last forever.** Think about that for a moment. Can you imagine having enough inheritance on earth that would never run out? That would be awesome! Unfortunately, things don't turn out that way with changes in the economy and the stock market. But we are promised what we inherit for heaven will never run out. This inheritance is our Living Hope: Jesus, who will always be with us. All he has is ours.

- **It will not be defiled.** Heaven is a place of purity and holiness. Nothing can tarnish our secure inheritance. As we live out our faith, we are sanctified every day. That is the ongoing work of the Holy Spirit in our lives to transform us into the image of Christ.

- **It will never fade**. I left a shirt on the patio to dry and forgot about it. The next day when I remembered, the sun had faded the color on one side. The shirt was ruined. But with all the benefits of Jesus as our inheritance, knowing he is the Light of the World assures us of an inheritance that will never fade.

With my house on the market and looking for another in a different location, I know I can't afford a mansion. But with my citizenship in heaven, I know the Lord prepares a mansion for me, a building not made with human hands, but by the very hand of God.

Believe this promise from the words of Jesus:

> *In my Father's house are many mansions: if it were not so, I would have told you. I go to prepare a place for you. And if I go and prepare a place for you, I will come again, and receive you unto myself; that where I am, there ye may be also. (John 14:2–3 KJV)*

Lord, I am so thankful for the preparations you are making for those who believe. I know nothing on earth can compare to my heavenly home and the inheritance you have waiting for me. I am blessed. Amen.

Chapter Five

Holy Is He

*"Our Father, in heaven,
hallowed be your name."*

Even when our earthly fathers fail, God our Father in heaven never will. He is holy and his holiness does not allow it. But he can take the failures of a father on earth and use them for his good purpose. He can change the man and extend his love through him no matter the human failure.

God's name is holy and not to be profaned, meaning it is not to be used as an expression of disdain or as a curse word. Holy is who he is. The word "hallowed" means holy. When we pray, "hallowed be thy name," we are acknowledging the holiness of God. This is the place in our prayer where we begin to praise the Lord for his character.

His attributes are his alone, but his character can be ours as we grow in our relationship with him.

Give unto the Lord the glory due to His name;
Worship the Lord in the beauty of holiness.
(Psalm 29:2 NKJV)

We praise him first for *who* he is and now for *how* he is. His character is righteous and just. He is merciful, faithful, and full of love. He *is* love. His characteristics as Father can be developed into the lives of men who become fathers, yet they will never be perfect as our Father in heaven is perfect.

Daniel is a young pastor. I heard him speak as he talked about his relationship with his father. He talked about camping trips and conversations that developed him into the godly man he is today by teaching him how to love the Lord. He said that growing up, his father would ask him questions before bed. His father still asks him these questions today.

1. How much do I love you?

2. How long will I love you?

3. What can you do to make me stop loving you?

I think the reason those questions resonated with me is because my husband always said something like that to our grandson, Alex. He told him, "I love you and there is nothing you can do about it." When Alex told his granddaddy goodbye for the final time, he repeated those words of love to him. It touched my heart to see love reciprocated this way.

That is how God loves us and there is nothing we can do about it. The difference is God is ever-present, surrounding us with his love. He will never leave us. Even though it may seem to our grandsons that their grandaddy left them, it is only temporary. They will see him again as they believe in the Lord Jesus Christ and have their place in heaven secured.

Daniel's message was about love. The love of God and the love of his father. What makes his story unique is that his parents were divorced for a reason deemed as failure. You hear so many stories of children from divorced parents where the dad simply disappeared from their lives. But this father did not desert his son. His love relationship was expressed in an act of the will to set aside his failures and desires to pour into his son unconditional love.

What a beautiful picture of God the Father and Jesus his Son. God did not desert his Son when he came to earth in the form of a man. God poured his will and purpose into Jesus that he would sacrifice his will and his life for you and me. Why? Because God loves us and wants a relationship with us that could only be accomplished by the shedding of blood to atone for sin. Jesus shed his blood on the cross for us in that while we were still sinners, He died for us.

If you are a parent, the time, love, and godly training you pour into your children now will reap godly results as they grow into adults. The Bible says to train up a child in the way they should go, and they will not depart from it. The training and conversations Daniel received from his father are what sparked the desire within him for seminary and becoming a pastor.

What a difference love makes for our children. Sadly, not all children receive this kind of love. Unfortunately, I am one. It was not until my husband and I married that I experienced and witnessed the kind of love God purposed for families as I watched his family live out their faith. I knew I wanted what they had but didn't know how to get it until someone I worked with pointed me to Jesus.

Prior to receiving Christ as Savior and learning to live according to God's Word, I was a young mom who failed at being a parent, but I never stopped loving my family. Parents have a responsibility to teach their children about the love of God the Father whether they are divorced or remain together, but I didn't know how. Not knowing Jesus early in life, and not taking our children to church is costly, and I paid the price.

For those children who do not receive love at home, and for adults who struggle as a result, God is watching. He sees the empty place in your heart, and he longs to fill it. He loves you and has provided a way for his love to be in you through Jesus.

Do not give up. Do not lose heart. God the Father makes a way when there seems to be no way. He would love for you to understand he is your heavenly Father. He can love you like no earthly father can and will not leave you. He is with you even now. You can trust him even when your trust in a father or mother has been shattered.

In the holy perfection of God, his is the love that reaches deep into our soul to fill the heart when we have an absentee father or mother. Our heavenly Father is never absent. He is present all around us and surrounds us with his love from perfect holiness.

> *Holy, holy, holy is the Lord of hosts;*
> *The whole earth is full of His glory!*
> *(Isaiah 6:3 NKJV)*

If you are an adult who has not received love from a father on earth, look to your heavenly Father to fill the needs of your heart. In his holiness, he will not turn you away.

Lord, you are my Lord and God. But more than that, you are the Father I have longed for. Thank you for loving me despite my negative emotions toward others. I claim you as my one and only way to enter heaven through Jesus Christ. Amen.

Chapter Six

Your Kingdom Come

"Our Father, in heaven,
hallowed be your name.
Your kingdom come."

In the prayer Jesus taught the disciples, the first few phrases were all about God. They give an example of what it means to praise him. But beginning with Matthew 6:10, the focus changes from praise to petition. A petition is an appeal to God as our authority. "Your kingdom come" is the first example of petition. Jesus taught us to pray, "Your kingdom come."

What is God's kingdom? It is the spiritual realm over which God reigns as King, and it is the fulfillment of God's will on earth. This phrase refers to the reign of Christ in the hearts and lives of believers. It is a call to do our part in serving the Lord in a way that draws others to him. We see the kingdom grow by simply doing what Jesus did on earth—telling others about God and the way to heaven. When we pray, "Your kingdom come," we are asking for revival across the land. This can occur as our lives reflect the love of Christ by sharing the gospel in the way we speak and live.

Because my husband and I chose ministry over career, we were always waiting for God's provision. When it came, it would always be just enough to last until the next time. Therefore, in the eyes of man, we looked like failures. But based on what was said when my husband passed away, I knew he was not only a success in God's eyes, but received many crowns when he entered heaven. I was overwhelmed with the hundreds of people who posted on social media and sent cards talking about the difference he made in their lives. He had a spirit of gentleness, kindness, compassion, and love for others. Lives were changed because of his service to the Lord as a chaplain. He led people to the saving grace of God through Christ. He talked some out of taking their own lives and sat with those who were hurting from loss until they were ready to talk. That sweet man had a calming presence in crisis. But most important, he prayed for them. He was expanding God's kingdom on earth and never realized the difference he was making.

Messages included: "Gene's profound faith—leaning fast into the arms of his Savior—is what so endeared him to me. Witnessing his expectant prayers to the Father for provision and seeing the Father answer was a huge testimony to us. Gene truly finished well and kept the faith. He has already heard, 'Well done, my good and faithful servant.'" And others: "Gene's ministry and heart for the Lord will be impacting lives for eternity...." "He was a godly man who had an everlasting impact on my life." I love these, but the one that touched me most is what our grandson, Bryan said: "I am proud to be his grandson. He impacted me spiritually more than anyone."

I share these as an example of what it means to live a life as a servant of the Lord in praying and living for the kingdom of God. Serving his purpose for drawing near to Christ in a way that others want to know him too. Praying for God's kingdom to come is asking for revival, peace, and unity among people and nations.

Therefore, when we pray, "Your kingdom come," we can make it personal.

Lord, help me to serve you in a way that expands your kingdom on earth in preparation for your kingdom to come in heaven. Grant me the wisdom to know what to do and say to make a difference in the lives of others. Teach me how to live a godly life.

So, what have we learned so far?

- Our Father is all-knowing, everywhere present all the time, and all power belongs to him alone.
- In heaven: Our Father is in heaven and our citizenship is heaven. We are just passing through this time on earth.
- Hallowed be thy name: Our Father is holy and is working to transform our lives to one of holiness no matter our past.

- Your kingdom come: begins the series of requests. We are asking for revival in our hearts and in the hearts of others that this world would find peace.

At this point, practice a prayer with what you have learned so far. What will you pray for first that will open the heart of God to you and draw you into his presence? Write the prayer to remember.

Chapter Seven

Your Will Be Done

*"Our Father, in heaven,
hallowed be your name.
Your kingdom come,
Your will be done."*

What happens when we want something so badly, it's all we can think about? The heart wants what the heart wants to the point of ratcheting up our anxiety and hindering everything else we do. We pray about it, ask for it, and want it right now. And when God doesn't answer our prayer for what we want, we become discouraged and give up on God. But as we desire something and pray about it, there is a component of the prayer that must be added—to pray for God's will in the ask.

It is not an easy decision to pray God's will over our own. But Jesus did. When he was in the garden before going to the cross, he asked that the cup pass from him. Yet not his will but God's will be done. Why did he pray in that way? Because he knew human suffering would take place in his body, but he also knew his mission and purpose.

He suffered for us so we could have access to the Father through his sacrifice.

And going a little farther he fell on his face and prayed, saying, "My Father, if it be possible, let this cup pass from me; nevertheless, not as I will, but as you will." (Matthew 26:39)

Notice Jesus said, "if it be possible." He knew all things are possible with God so he gave up his own power in that moment because he also knew God's will is for a purpose, even when it hurts.

In the verse above, "will" from "not as I will" is to wish or desire. This is what we do in our human nature. We wish or desire something to be done. But praying God's will be done is to acknowledge God as personal with a response that is personal to you, but beneficial in ways you cannot see. It is surrendering our wants, wishes, and desires to God's plan and purpose. His will is perfect, gracious, and a determined resolve.

> "God's will is what God wants—when, where, and how he wants it. Those who are part of God's family are to follow God's rules. He's sovereign, and he'll accomplish his purposes with you or without you. The question is, will you get to take part in it? Remember, he's not limited to our obedience."

Praying for God's will in our lives means giving up our own desires to accomplish God's purpose. According to Hebrews 13:21, God equips us with what we need to carry out his plan. He works in us through Jesus to do those tasks that are pleasing to him.

As pastor and author Tony Evans wrote, "God's will is what God wants—when, where, and how he wants it. Those who are part of God's family are to follow God's rules. He's sovereign, and he'll accomplish his purposes with you or without you. The question is, will you get to take part in it? Remember, he's not limited to our obedience."[2]

If we follow our will rather than God's for a purpose he gives us, he will use someone else, and we miss the blessing.

How do we know God's will for us? The Bible lists things that are definite for everyone.

1. **It is God's will that none should perish** but all come to the saving knowledge of Jesus Christ. "The Lord is not slow to fulfill his promise as some count slowness, but is patient toward you, not wishing that any should perish, but that all should reach repentance" (II Peter 3:9).

    "For God so loved the world, that he gave his only Son, that whoever believes in him should not perish but have eternal life" (John 3:16). The word "should" indicates we have a choice: perish or have eternal life.

2. **It is God's will that we understand the love of Jesus and come to him by faith** as a small child. "At that time Jesus declared, 'I thank you, Father, Lord of heaven and earth, that you have hidden these things from the wise and understanding and revealed them to little

children; yes, Father, for such was your gracious will'" (Matthew 11:25–26).

It still amazes me to hear and see how God uses innocent little children to speak of him. When Abigail started going to preschool, she wanted to dress herself. One morning she walked into the living room and her mother said, "Well, who did you get all dolled up for?"

"God."

"How did you know to do that?"

"He told me."

"How did he tell you?"

"Right here in my heart." (She placed her hand over her heart.)

And then Fallon, while my husband was ill, loved to talk to him on the phone. One day she said, "Grandaddy, I pray for you." She was two at the time and talked like an adult but in that sweet, two-year-old voice, she prayed.

Our hearts melted when we heard the voices of these precious children. God refers to us as his children. We may come to him without knowledge of what the Bible tells us. But he reveals himself to us, for that is his will. As we talk to him, he loves what we say and speaks to our hearts.

3. **It is God's will that we work, not to please people, but from the heart to please God** as we serve, doing his will. Ephesians 6:6 reminds us our obedience is "not by the way of eye-service, as people-pleasers, but as bondservants of Christ, doing the will of God from the heart."

4. **It is God's will that our minds be renewed to discern the will of God.** "Do not be conformed to this world, but be transformed by the renewal of your mind, that by testing you may discern what is the will of God, what is good and acceptable and perfect" (Romans 12:2).

As we grow in our faith and pray, we begin to know the difference between what we once thought was right, but realize now, it is not. So often, when we are not familiar with the Bible, we do things we don't realize go against God's will for us. Once we understand the will of God is for our minds to be transformed to his way of thinking, those actions can no longer be part of our lives. For example, knowing God created sex for marriage motivates us to keep ourselves for our spouse. It is a gift for us to enjoy in the marriage relationship between a man and a woman.

1 Thessalonians 4:3–4 makes it clear that his will is to abstain from sex outside the bounds of marriage. "For this is the will of God, your sanctification: that you abstain from sexual immorality; that each one of you

know how to control his own body in holiness and honor, not in the passion of lust like the Gentiles who do not know God."

Remember, sanctification is the ongoing work of God through the Holy Spirit. If we are paying attention to God's work in our lives, immorality should not be an option.

5. **It is God's will that we live according to his Word.** (See James 1:22; Ephesians 4:1–2.) James 1:22 reminds us to "Be doers of the word, and not hearers only, deceiving yourselves." And Ephesians 4:1–2 tells us to "walk in a manner worthy of the calling to which you have been called, with all humility and gentleness, with patience, bearing with one another in love."

The humility, gentleness, and patience we are called to in Ephesians 4:2 are characteristics of God that can be developed in us as we grow in our faith.

6. **It is God's will that our whole heart belongs to him.** All of me for all of him. David wrote in the Psalms, "I give thanks to you, O Lord my God, with my whole heart, and I will glorify your name forever" (Psalm 86:12 ESV). This verse follows the psalmist asking the Lord to teach him to walk in God's truth. It is followed with the psalmist acknowledging God's steadfast love toward him exhibited in his deliverance. David is teachable, committed, and thankful. This is how we show God our whole heart belongs to him.

As we practice these things, it becomes easier and more common for us to pray his will be done rather than our own. When Jesus prayed in that way, his human body desired for the cup of suffering to pass from him. But in his deity, he knew the will of God must be done for the purpose of his kingdom drawing near to him.

What is something you have wanted for a long time but has not come to pass? What can you learn from Jesus' example to help as you pray for it? Ask yourself: Is this God's will for me to have this new job, or new house, or marry this person? He will give the direction you need.

What is it you want more than anything? Write it below. Then write a prayer based on what you have learned from this chapter. *God, not my will, but your will be done in my life.*

When someone you love leaves you and goes to heaven to be with Jesus, it is a time of both sorrow and joy. Joy, because God's kingdom in heaven is one of peace and rejoicing. There is no more pain or suffering. No more tears. But it is also a time of sorrow for those left behind on earth because we've experienced their love and loved in return.

We may ask, was this God's will? Then we read that God knew the number of our days before there was one of them. He knows the day we will leave this earth, but this doesn't mean he caused the death. Accidents happen, disease invades the body, murders occur perpetrated by those with evil intent. But what people mean for evil, God can turn around for good. The good in these events is heaven. Sorrow may blame God, but joy says your loved one is no longer struggling. God makes right what is wrong in this world.

Praying "your kingdom come, your will be done on earth as it is in heaven" is asking for revival, peace, and unity among people and nations. Use this time to pray for those who need to know Jesus, that lives would be transformed, peace would reign, and the world be united in peace. God's kingdom in heaven is so much greater than his kingdom on earth.

Surrendering simply means to let go of what we think is right, and let God take control of our life. He has the wheel. We are the passengers going where he takes us. There is not a sample prayer for this chapter. Write your own prayer of surrendering your will to God's will.

Chapter Eight

Daily Bread

"Our Father, in heaven,
hallowed be your name.
Your kingdom come,
Your will be done,
on earth as it is in heaven.
Give us this day our daily bread."

When money is tight and bills stack up, we tend to worry. I confess, I was once a worrywart! But God taught me how to be worry-free. The first verse I memorized as a believer is Matthew 6:33: "Seek first the kingdom of God and his righteousness, and all these things will be added to you." What things?

We find the answer in verse 25 of Matthew 6, talking about our provisions for life. What we eat, where we live, the clothes we wear, and any other tangible needs we have. God is faithful to meet our needs. Notice, I did not say our wants, but what we need to sustain us day by day.

Jesus said not to be anxious about what we eat, drink, or put on our bodies. Life is more than food and clothing.

He made it known that God provides. Therefore, we have direction to ask for our daily needs by faith, believing they will be provided. Since Jesus told us not to worry, that means it is not God who causes worry. It is not from him. Therefore, we need to ask him to replace our worry with his peace.

God gives our daily bread. It is not only his presence, but basics for daily needs. "The bread is to keep us going forward, day by day. It is for each new day so the mind may conform to Christ's warning against anxiety for tomorrow."[3]

To bake bread, we need a combination of ingredients to create something that could not exist without the mixture. In the physical sense, we need daily nourishment to sustain life on earth. Jesus is the Bread of Life and in the spiritual sense, we need him every day. He contains all the ingredients we need to live according to God's will. He is the grace of God who gave himself for us that we can enjoy fellowship with him, and he with us.

> *"The bread is to keep us going forward, day by day. It is for each new day so the mind may conform to Christ's warning against anxiety for tomorrow."*

In the Old Testament, bread called shewbread was not cut. It was broken every Sabbath day and consecrated for the Lord. How interesting that God gave this instruction to Moses knowing that one day, the body of Jesus would be broken for us to be set apart for the Lord. God told Moses the people were to: "Set the bread of the Presence on the table before me regularly" (Exodus 25:30). The "Presence" in this verse represents the Lord himself. Moving forward into the New Testament and the night before Jesus was crucified, he and the disciples gathered for his last supper. When he prayed before the meal, Scripture said this: "And he took bread, and when he had given thanks, he broke it and gave it to them, saying, 'This is my body which is given for you. Do this in remembrance of me'" (Luke 22:19).

Just as the broken bread in the Old Testament was preparing to set Israel apart for God, the bread broken by Jesus was preparing the world for setting ourselves apart for him, the Bread of Life. That is what being consecrated means—to be holy, set apart for the Lord. It is why we serve what we call the Lord's Supper, or communion, periodically in church. But if a person has not used that time to cleanse themselves through prayer, and never committed their life to Christ, participating is meaningless for them. The bread represents the body of Christ, and the drink represents the blood of Christ on the cross. Our participation indicates we are remembering what Jesus did for us on the cross. If you don't believe it, you should not take the bread and drink.

But when you see this foretold throughout Scripture and took place thousands of years earlier, it is easier to understand God's plan for our redemption through Jesus. He is all we need for life and holiness. All he is combined is called the Bread of Life. Therefore, we pray, "Give us this day our daily bread" with confidence knowing God is Jehovah-Jireh, the Lord Who Provides.

As Jesus prepared the disciples for sharing the gospel after he left earth, he performed many miracles, each one a lesson. In John 6:1–14, we read about the miracle of five loaves and two fish. Jesus was teaching on the side of the mountain to a large crowd who followed him, approximately five thousand people. He knew they were hungry and there was a discussion with the doubting disciples about how to feed that many people. Andrew knew of a boy with five loaves and two fish, yet he asked, "But what are they to feed so many?"

> *"Even though she is not mentioned in Scripture, I imagine it was a mom who packed the little boy's lunch that day, never knowing how Jesus would use it to feed thousands."*

But Jesus took the bread and fish and distributed to all who were seated, as much as they wanted. When they had eaten their fill, Jesus told the disciples, "Gather up the leftover fragments, that nothing may be lost." (Now comes my favorite part of the story.) When they did what Jesus said, there was enough left over for twelve baskets. How many disciples? Twelve! Jesus not only miraculously provided daily bread for the crowd, but for those who served him as well. He knew there would be enough.

In the physical sense, I have personally experienced his provision in miraculous ways since the day of my salvation and in the ministry. Like many small parachurch ministries, ours struggled financially to provide for staff and operations. Our stance was to take care of clients first, staff next, and if any was left for our salary, great. If not, we continued to pray and serve the Lord, trusting his provisions would come. God always met our needs. He puts it in the hearts of people to serve him through giving, some for service and some for making provision for service. We are so thankful for all who gave, making it possible for us to help those who were in trauma and disaster as well as supporting staff. God uses people to make provision for those who serve. You may be one who serves by giving or one who serves by doing, but both desires are a gift of God.

A friend in our church, Ivy, makes the most delicious homemade bread I have ever tasted. It is her way of giving and serving. She is like the mom of the little boy from John 6:9. Dr. Jack Graham, senior pastor of Prestonwood Baptist Church, said this in a sermon: "Even though she is not mentioned in Scripture, I imagine it was a mom who packed the little boy's lunch that day, never knowing how Jesus would use it to feed thousands." When we give, we don't always know how God will use it. He uses the obedience of people to provide for others.

But even after the miracle, the people called him a prophet. They still did not understand he was the long-awaited Messiah among them. In verse 26, Jesus told them they were only seeking him because they ate their fill of loaves. It is like they were thinking, what will he do for us next? But Jesus knew their thoughts and said,

> *"Do not work for the food that perishes,*
> *But for the food that endures to eternal life,*

> *which the Son of Man will give to you.*
> *For on him God the Father has set his seal."*
> *Then they said to him, "What must we do to be*
> *doing the works of God?"*
> *Jesus answered them, "This is the work of God,*
> *That you believe in him whom he has sent."*
> *(John 6:27–29)*

> *Truly, truly, I say to you,*
> *whoever believes has eternal life.*
> *I am the bread of life.*
> *(John 6:47–48)*

Many stories of provision came from those years of ministry with my husband, but one I will never forget. A group of our volunteers were serving in Grenada following a hurricane that devastated the island. Living conditions were primitive. They cooked and ate around a campfire while there. After two weeks, they gathered one night to eat another pot of rice and beans. As the chaplain prayed, he said, "Lord, we thank you for our daily meal but we sure would like some meat." About that time, a chicken ran between his legs and jumped into the pot. I'm not sure God caused the chicken to do that, but it was the comic relief needed in a moment of lack and discouragement. I wish I had asked what they did next. Did they pluck and eat the chicken? We have laughed about that story for years. Perhaps the Lord was doing what he did for the Israelites when they complained about eating manna (bread) every day. He gave until they were sick of it. And I imagine the thought of eating rice and beans after a dirty chicken jumped in was enough to make anyone sick.

As a new widow (first time I have said that in reference to me), I don't worry about how I will take care of finances. We experienced God's provision all our married life, and I know he will not stop now. The year before Gene went to heaven, I prayed God would provide a job I could do at home that would help with our needs. Without my knowledge, a friend recommended me to a company that was exactly what I needed and prayed for. I got the job and love it. As a result of God's faithfulness to us, I have not worried. I fully trust God for my daily bread as I pray and lean into him and continue to follow where he leads. I desire his will over my own because I know he knows what is best for me.

We learn from the story of the five loaves and two fish that Jesus will multiply what we bring to him. What we give for his service is used to provide for others. When we have anxiety, give it to him and he will give peace. When we have a loss and are grieving, give it to him and he will give comfort. When we have financial resources and give back ten percent to the Lord, he will multiply it for service to accomplish his purpose. Whatever you give to help others does not go unnoticed by the Lord and your reward in heaven will be great.

When was the last time you trusted God for your daily bread? Or think about your motive for giving a financial gift to someone or to church. Was it to please God, out of obligation, or to please a person?

Father in heaven, you are great and greatly praised. Thank you for using others to help us as we go about your work serving you. And as I pray, "Give us this day our daily bread," I do so with confidence knowing my daily bread is Jesus, the giver of life. I trust that through him, provisions are made for my life. Amen.

Chapter Nine

Forgive Us

"Our Father, in heaven,
hallowed be your name.
Your kingdom come,
Your will be done,
on earth as it is in heaven.
Give us this day our daily bread,
and forgive us our debts."

No one likes to confess to others the wrong things they have done. They are trespasses against God and his Word, and probably others. We have a conscience that tells us the difference between right and wrong. Yet we do what we want anyway. Our conscience is a knowing within and the witness to our conduct. It is a "process of thought that distinguishes what it considers morally good or bad, commending the good, condemning the bad, and so prompting to do the former, and avoid the latter."[4]

Therefore, if we ignore our conscience and do what we want even though we know it is bad, that is sin. It is this sin Jesus is talking about when he taught the disciples to pray, "Forgive us our debts." A debt is something that must be paid back. Jesus' blood on the cross is the payment for our sin, buying us back to a relationship with God. Sin separates us from God. It puts a barrier between us because God cannot look upon the face of sin. He wants us to come to him pure and holy as he is holy, which is not possible without a relationship with him through Jesus to wash us clean.

What Jesus did is called redemption. What does this look like? When I was twelve years old, the newspaper boy was the same age. Each afternoon when I returned from school, I would twirl my baton in the yard. When he delivered the paper, he would stop his motor scooter at the curb, and we would talk. In those days, if you liked each other, you said you were going steady. All that meant was letting your classmates know you had a boyfriend or girlfriend. It really meant nothing at all.

But one day, he gave me a ring that was clunky and ugly (in my opinion). I put it on a chain around my neck and proudly showed it to my high school brother. He immediately recognized it for what it was and told our daddy. They recognized it as a high school senior ring and knew the owner by the initials. The owner of the ring turned out to be a friend of another brother, who was a senior. They called him and told him we had the ring, and he could pick it up.

All I wanted to do was hide in my room in shame and embarrassment, but Daddy made me come out and give the ring to the owner. As I held out my hand, tears ran down my face. But when I looked up into his face, all I saw was compassion. As he took the ring, he reached into his back pocket and pulled out a twenty-dollar bill which he gave to me. He bought back something that already belonged to him.

It wasn't until years later when I became a believer that I realized God had given me a perfect picture of redemption. That is what Jesus did for us. He paid the price for our sin with his blood to buy us back for God so that we belong to him. Sin separates us until we willingly open our hearts to receive what Jesus offers: the fullness of forgiveness made possible by his sacrifice on the cross for you and me. What a Savior!

When we pray, we should always be willing to confess our sin to our heavenly Father. He knows it already because he is all-knowing. But acknowledging our sin is the first step toward forgiveness. The Holy Spirit of God tells us what is good and what is not. When our actions are not good, we have an unsettled feeling within. We do not feel peace. Take that as a sign to ask God to reveal what sin is in your heart that you may not be aware of. Ask for forgiveness, then go and sin no more.

If you feel far from God, perhaps there is something hindering you from sensing his presence and knowing when he speaks a word to you. If that is the case, there is a sample prayer below to get you started with a blank space for your confession.

Lord Jesus, thank you for your forgiveness of past, present, and future sin. But for me, old habits that may be considered sinful are hard to break, and I long for your presence. I confess to you today that I _____ and ask your forgiveness once again, that I will be clean before you with nothing hindering me from knowing your presence, peace, and instruction for me. In your name I pray, Amen.

Chapter Ten

As We Forgive

"Our Father, in heaven,
hallowed be your name.
Your kingdom come,
Your will be done,
on earth as it is in heaven.
Give us this day our daily bread,
and forgive us our debts,
as we also have forgiven our debtors."

Have you ever given a gift you resented giving or thought it would buy forgiveness? Jesus talked about that in Matthew 5:22: "But I say to you that everyone who is angry with his brother will be liable to judgment; whoever insults his brother will be liable to the council; and whoever says, 'You fool!' will be liable to the hell of fire."

Those are harsh words, but the point Jesus was making is to deal with our anger and stop with insults and name-calling. Get right with others before expecting God to answer our prayer asking for forgiveness. And when someone comes to us asking us to forgive them for a wrong done, we are to give it freely just as Jesus does for us.

Asking God to forgive us when we are holding a grudge against someone without forgiving them is like saying, "I deserve forgiveness; they do not." It puts us in the place of being judgmental. According to James 4:12, "There is only one lawgiver and judge, he who is able to save and destroy. But who are you to judge your neighbor?"

In Jesus' Sermon on the Mount, he told what to do about judging others. "If you are offering your gift at the altar and there remember that your brother has something against you, leave your gift there before the altar and go. First be reconciled to your brother and then come and offer your gift" (Matthew 5:23–24).

Our money given on Sunday at church does not buy our forgiveness or reconciliation with God. That price was paid by Jesus' sacrifice on the cross. When we give out of resentment or obligation, or have anger in our heart toward someone, the gift is tainted with unforgiveness. Doing a good deed does not bring forgiveness. We are to forgive others before we present our offering to the Lord. A gift from the heart is worth more than silver or gold. It is an indication of our love and commitment to Jesus. In fact, God desires our mercy and values it as worth more than our sacrifice (Matthew 9:13). Mercy forgives. Mercy is love. The ritual of the Pharisees' sacrifice was not out of mercy, but for show. Saying we forgive someone so we can look good is not sincere because there is no mercy or love shown. It is not true forgiveness.

In the Bible, a sacrificial gift was given for several purposes.

- It was presented as an expression of honor.
- It was presented for support of the ministry and the needs of the poor.
- It was presented to God as an offering.
- It was given in celebration.

But the gift was not always money, silver, or gold. For application today, the Bible tells us our praise and worship are gifts to God. His gift to us is salvation given by his mercy and grace. It was a sacrifice.

There may be occasions when we serve the Lord that we must sacrifice something else to do so. Maybe we had tickets to a ball game or concert. Then we remember we were supposed to help a person in the church with their lawn or take them somewhere because they can't drive. Giving up the game or concert is going to be a sacrifice for us, not only of time, but the cost of the tickets. But service is our gift to God. Part of that service is forgiveness. When we forgive others, it may not change them, but it gives us freedom from bitterness toward them.

The promise we have from Jesus to his disciples is this: "For this is my blood of the covenant, which is poured out for many for the forgiveness of sins" (Matthew 26:28).

Lord, thank you for making redemption possible to cleanse me from my sin no matter my past. Thank you for the sacrifice you made to forgive me, giving strength and courage to forget the past and press on toward the upward call of Jesus. Today I will live as one forgiven, turning to you in repentance and trusting you for guidance day to day. Give me what I need in wisdom and opportunity to forgive others as you have forgiven me. Amen.

Chapter Eleven

Lead Us Not into Temptation

"Our Father, in heaven,
hallowed be your name.
Your kingdom come,
Your will be done,
on earth as it is in heaven.
Give us this day our daily bread,
and forgive us our debts,
as we also have forgiven our debtors.
And lead us not into temptation."

There is a piece of cherry pie in the kitchen. I'm working but can't stop thinking about that piece of pie. I don't want it to go to waste. In fact, I want it, but don't need it. Yesterday when I ate a piece I gained a pound. Can I resist the temptation to eat it for only a moment's pleasure and suffering later? Yes, I can!

Temptations come in many ways and always have since the days of Adam and Eve. They are desires to do something that is wrong or unwise. Cherry pie was unwise for me at that time. Once we give in to the desire, allowing the temptation to become action that grieves the Holy Spirit (see Ephesians 4:30), we have taken a step away from God. This becomes an obstacle to our closeness with God, causing prayer to be difficult for us because we allowed something else to get in the way of our thoughts.

The need for confession and forgiveness is necessary to restore closeness with God. It is not that he becomes distant from us, but we become distant from him. Just as I hid in my room as a twelve-year-old not wanting to face the ring redeemer, we too try to hide from God. (I'm not saying cherry pie obstructed my relationship with God, just using it as an example of temptation.)

God told Adam not to eat from a certain tree in the Garden of Eden, but the crafty serpent (Satan), tempted Eve by disputing God's Word. She not only took and ate fruit from the forbidden tree but gave it to Adam and he ate. In the moment of believing a lie, they did according to their own desires and innocence was destroyed. They hid from God in guilt. But God called to them, and they confessed (see Genesis 3).

When we give in to what we want rather than what God wants for us, there will be consequences. The consequences given to Adam and Eve have been handed down through the generations. Women still have pain in childbirth and work is still a difficult struggle. We are all in need of a Savior because of the first couple.

God made provision for their redemption by the shed blood of an animal to provide covering for their nakedness. Their eyes had been opened and they were ashamed (see Genesis 3:21). Throughout the Old Testament, we find animal sacrifice was never enough. The blood of animals for atonement had to be accomplished every year. That is why God sent his Son, Jesus, as the divine sacrifice to cover our sin and cleanse us from all unrighteousness once for all. His one-time sacrifice covers us forever. Through him we have eternal life with our place in heaven secured. However, his sacrifice requires our faith and trust, believing in him as our Savior. God has given us all a choice to receive him or reject him. His sacrifice does not cover those who reject him unless they turn to him in faith believing.

When we receive forgiveness at the point of our commitment to Christ Jesus for salvation, our place in heaven is secured. But because we don't always do what is right, the wrong we do can get in the way of relationship. This is why there is need for confession to God with a commitment not to repeat the wrong action.

The phrase in the Lord's Prayer, "and lead us not into temptation," is an interesting phrase for Jesus to use because James tells us God does not tempt anyone.

> *Let no one say when he is tempted, "I am being*
> *tempted by God," for God cannot be tempted*
> *with evil, and he himself tempts no one. But*
> *each person is tempted when he is lured and*
> *enticed by his own desire. Then desire when it*

> *has conceived gives birth to sin, and sin when it*
> *is fully grown brings forth death.*
> *(James 1:13–15) [The death spoken of is spiritual*
> *separation from God.]*

Do you see the sequence of events? Temptation leads to a decision as we face our own desires. When giving in to our desires over what is right, sin is conceived. The more we sin, the further we grow from God.

For someone new to faith, the verse in Matthew and these verses in James seem to contradict one another. When you see something like this, it is important to dig further to gain understanding. For clarification, we discover from the original Greek language of the New Testament that the verse in James 1:13 is talking about temptations arising within us from uncontrolled desires. These do not come from God. He does not tempt us from within to turn away from him and his ways. We are tempted by the one who wants to draw us away from the goodness of God. When the moment of temptation comes, we need to ask ourselves, "Will I remain faithful to God, or will I do what I want to do?

But the temptation mentioned in the Lord's Prayer indicates testing. This is talking about those circumstances that occur outside of us and are beyond our control. When we look at James 1:2–4, we can see the difference.

> *Count it all joy, my brothers, when you meet*
> *trials of various kinds, for you know that the*
> *testing of your faith produces steadfastness. And*

let steadfastness have its full effect, that you
may be perfect and complete, lacking in nothing.
(James 1:2–4)

Even though God does not tempt believers to sin, he does sometimes allow circumstances to test our faith. When trials come, we are strengthened by them as we pray through them trusting God for the outcome no matter what it is. Therefore, we are to pray to be delivered from them, so we won't be tempted to give up on God and take a wrong path simply because it seems easier.

To prove the deity of Jesus, God allowed the Spirit to lead him to a place of temptation (testing) in the wilderness. This is important to remember as we find ourselves in a wilderness place of grief, loss, financial stress, being overextended, discouragement, and circumstances beyond our control. Ask the Lord if your faith is being tested. Ask him to protect you from falling into despair in your weak moments. It is when our emotional defenses are depleted that the devil strikes to cause us to fall into sin. Don't give up on God. He knows what we can handle and will not allow more than we can bear.

We find strength in the example of seeing how Jesus proved himself on the mountain in the wilderness. Satan tempted him in his hunger with bread. Then he offered the power of kingdoms and mocked him regarding what God said about angels lifting him up.

With everything the tempter offered, Jesus rebuked him with God's Word, beginning with the phrase, "It is written…" followed by what God said. Satan wanted Jesus to fall down and worship him. With that, Jesus said to him, "Be gone, Satan! For it is written, you shall worship the Lord your God and him only shall you serve" (Matthew 4:1–11). When confronted with God's Word, the devil left him.

From this story, we find the importance of reading and knowing God's Word to use as a weapon against the enemy of our soul when we are tempted to go against God's purpose for us. We begin to realize the necessity of planting the words of the Bible in our hearts to call upon when we feel tempted. Jesus is our strength and deliverer. When in doubt or temptation, ask for deliverance.

The testing of believers is to prove our faithfulness to God during difficulties. What Satan offers are lies. He tempts with what he does not own. What he did then, he does today by offering get-rich-quick schemes or something we desire but don't have the ability to obtain. I play games on my phone on occasion, but I only download the free ones. Lately I have noticed more and more of them are tempting people to play for money, showing examples of others winning big dollars. Don't believe the lie. This is a temptation that can quickly turn to addiction and the loss of your money. God, and God alone, is our provider. He gives according to our needs but not necessarily according to our desires. But as we grow in our faith, our desires begin to match up with his.

The purpose of the testing of our faith is to produce spiritual maturity and should therefore be counted as joy.

With the test comes a promise. "Blessed is the man who remains steadfast under trial, for when he has stood the test he will receive the crown of life, which God has promised to those who love him" (James 1:12). These crowns are the reward we receive in heaven to cast at the feet of Jesus in worship. I don't know about you, but I don't want to be one who has no crown to present to Jesus when the time comes.

Therefore, I pray for strength to carry me through the trials of life.

"Lead us not into temptation" is the same as saying, "Do not lead me into difficulties that test my faith, but deliver me from the dishonor and disrespect that lurks in the circumstances."

Our Father in heaven, thank you for your Word to remember and repeat when being tempted within. And in times of testing, I pray for the strength to endure and prove my faithfulness. Deliver me from what I should not do and teach me what is right, good, and pleasing to you as my heavenly Father. In Jesus' name I pray, Amen.

Chapter Twelve

Deliver Us from Evil

"Our Father, in heaven,
hallowed be your name.
Your kingdom come,
Your will be done,
on earth as it is in heaven.
Give us this day our daily bread,
and forgive us our debts,
as we also have forgiven our debtors.
And lead us not into temptation,
but deliver us from evil."

Flames leapt from buildings as rioters threw torches into windows. Fights broke out in the streets and gunshots were heard. People were killed. No, this was not an action movie. This is real life we never expected to see in our lifetime. Who stirred up the civil unrest in our nation? It is not God's fault. It is the evil heart of humanity. People listening to voices with evil intent are participating in atrocities that were once unspeakable. Riots, murders, rapes, and human trafficking of young people including children are taking place every day. How have we come to this?

When we think of evil, things occurring outside of us come to mind. But what Jesus taught in his prayer, "deliver us from evil," means something different. He was teaching his followers to ask to be delivered from moral deficiency within us. The evil he is speaking of is the tendency of people to do what is contrary to the will of God in their thoughts and actions.

In the Old Testament, godly kings ruled according to the wisdom they received from God. Then another generation would come along and rule according to what was right in their own eyes, and a nation would fall. We are living in a generation of people doing what seems right to them without regard for God, others, or property. We are being destroyed from the inside out. When we pray to be delivered from moral deficiency within ourselves, we can also pray that those who are morally deficient will turn from their wicked ways and turn to God. The psalmist in Psalm 141:3–4 and 8–10 prayed for protection from doing evil that is contrary to God's will. He then prayed for protection from the traps of the wicked.

Without intervention from God through our prayers today, things don't look promising for the future of our nation. Turning to God and praying for peace and unity are the answers to restoration.

> *If my people who are called by my name*
> *humble themselves, and pray and seek my face*

> *and turn from their wicked ways, then I will*
> *hear from heaven and will forgive their sin and*
> *heal their land. (II Chronicles 7:14)*

God was speaking to Solomon in the above verse. We can apply these words by acknowledging that as believers, we are called by the name of Jesus. To humble ourselves means to bow before our holy God, putting ourselves under his authority. To turn is to come back to God and away from evil deeds of harm, mischief, and grievous ways. The word for this is "repentance." Turn ourselves around from what is destructive and turn to God for wisdom. Ask him if what we are doing is right and for the power to turn our lives around for good when we are wrong.

After God gave these instructions and promises in verse 14, he then gave a warning we need to pay attention to as well.

> *But if you turn aside and forsake my statutes*
> *and my commandments that I have set before*
> *you, and go and serve other gods and worship*
> *them, then I will pluck you up from my land*
> *that I have given you, and this house that I*
> *have consecrated for my name, I will cast out*
> *of my sight, and I will make it a proverb and a*
> *byword among all peoples. And at this house,*
> *which was exalted, everyone passing by will be*
> *astonished and say, "Why has the Lord done*
> *thus to this land and to this house?" Then they*
> *will say, 'Because they abandoned the Lord, the*

> *God of their fathers who brought them out of*
> *the land of Egypt, and laid hold on other gods*
> *and worshiped them and served them. Therefore,*
> *he has brought all this disaster on them."*
> *(II Chronicles 7:19–22)*

There are harsh consequences for turning away from God, for individuals and for nations. The founding fathers of this nation established religious freedom in the Constitution. A day of prayer, fasting, and humiliation was proclaimed by Samuel Huntington, Esquire (signer of the Declaration of Independence), while he served as Governor of Connecticut. The proclamation, issued on March 28, 1789, declared April 22, 1789, as a day of fasting, humiliation, and prayer.[5]

> Separation of church and state does not mean government leaders are to turn from God in how they rule.

Prayer and seeking God were part of establishing our nation. Therefore, the words of II Chronicles 7:14–22 are a message to take note of even today. When we pray for deliverance from evil in humility before the Lord, he answers as we turn from those areas of our lives that are not in keeping with his perfect will. This applies to every nation who seeks the Lord for how to rule in government. Separation of church and state does not mean government leaders are to turn from God in how they rule.

God is the ultimate ruler of heaven and earth. As we follow his leadership, we can be a united nation. Therefore, we pray "Deliver us from evil," so we can be a nation of peace, hope, and unity.

Lord, deliver me from any thoughts or actions that are leading me astray. Help me to be a godly example to those who do not know you and to those who come against our faith. As the psalmist prayed, may the words of my mouth and the meditations of my heart be pleasing to you. In the name of Jesus I pray, Amen.

Chapter Thirteen

For Thine Is the Kingdom - Summary

"Our Father, in heaven,
hallowed be your name.
Your kingdom come,
Your will be done,
on earth as it is in heaven.
Give us this day our daily bread,
and forgive us our debts,
as we also have forgiven our debtors.
And lead us not into temptation,
but deliver us from evil.
*For thine is the kingdom, and the power,
and the glory forever.
Amen."
(*This phrase is not in all translations, but is in the KJV)

Jesus' prayer begins and ends with praise to God, acknowledging his kingdom, power, and glory will last forever. Even when nations on earth fail and fall, God's kingdom never will. When we feel powerless, God's power never runs out. When nothing seems glorious to us, the glory of God is forever and ever. And one day, we will see him in all his glory.

In summary, the Lord's Prayer is broken down into six sections to help you as you are learning how to pray:

1. **Worship & Praise**
   a. Father
   b. Heaven
   c. Holy name

2. **God's Will**
   a. On earth – revival
   b. In heaven – believers
   c. Our lives – that none should perish

3. **Provision**
   a. What we eat
   b. What we wear
   c. Where we live

4. **Confession**
   a. Forgive us
   b. List sin
   c. Forgive others

5. **Guidance**
   a. How I live
   b. Where I hang out
   c. What I do

6. **Protection**
    a. From temptation
    b. From evil
    c. From making poor choices

7. **Amen**
    a. Means "so be it."

Hopefully, by now, you can recite the Lord's Prayer from memory. Now practice making it personal phrase by phrase. When you say, "Our Father," think of who he is to you. Think of worship as you recall his attributes.

- **Our Father,** thank you for (finish in a personal way acknowledging the awesome attributes of God).
- **Who is in heaven,** the place where (add your prayer notes).
- **Hallowed be your name.** (Think about what it means to be holy.)
- **Your kingdom come.** (Where is God's kingdom?)
- **Your will be done.** (Can you release your will to God's will for you?)
- **On earth as it is in heaven.** (What is God's will for you on earth and in heaven?)
- **Give us this day our daily bread.** (Are you worried about your needs? Thank God in confidence for his provision.)
- **And forgive us our debts.** (Confess your sins to God and seek forgiveness. Say them out loud to him.)

- **As we have also forgiven our debtors.** (Who do you need to forgive? Apply love and mercy to your forgiving spirit. Name the person.)
- **And lead us not into temptation.** (When you hold your thoughts captive to the obedience of Christ as the Bible says, your thoughts are his thoughts without being tempted to do things in contrast to God's will.)
- **But deliver us from evil.** (Ask God to guard your heart from moral deficiency, and to guard our nation from those with wicked intent.)
- **For thine is the kingdom and the power and the glory forever** (KJV). (Acknowledge God as the sovereign ruler of all.)

Using the model Jesus taught, and what you have learned through the book, write your prayer below as a reference point any time you feel yourself doubt the goodness of God. You can use the summary as a guide.

It is exciting to me for readers, especially those new to prayer, to begin their journey of faith and prayer. Reading messages from the Bible as they relate to how to pray can seem overwhelming. But please know God will not laugh at you. He will hear your prayer and encourage you along your spiritual journey. There is no other journey in life more important than the one of prayer, knowing you are in the presence of the Lord, and he listens to you as a Father to a son and daughter.

As Paul prayed for believers in Ephesus, I pray for you, that God may give you a spirit of wisdom and knowledge of him with your eyes open to know the hope of your calling and the immeasurable greatness of his power toward us who believe.

You can begin by reading the book of Psalms in the Bible. It is filled with prayers for every occasion. Also, read the book of John to learn more about Jesus and what he has done for us.

> *For God so loved the world,*
> *that he gave his only Son,*
> *that whoever believes in him*
> *shall not perish*
> *but have eternal life.*
> *(John 3:16)*

> *In my distress I called to the LORD,*
> *and he answered me.*
> *(Psalm 120:1)*

> *Do good, O LORD, to those who are good,*
> *and to those who are upright in their hearts!*
> *(Psalm 125:4)*

Conclusion

When I got on my knees by my bed to ask Jesus into my life, I will never forget the sense of urgency I felt to know more from the Bible. My husband and I were not attending church at the time, but I had a deep longing to find one where I could learn more about God. Shortly after, we received a postcard in the mail inviting us to attend a new mission church. We began to attend, and it was there I learned about a women's Bible study class. I joined the group and discovered for the first time that Bible study had homework. Through the class and homework, I began to know and understand who God is, how Jesus shed his blood on a cross to buy us back for God (redemption), and how to live as a believer. And most important, I learned how to pray.

I say all of this to encourage you as someone who may be new to faith, prayer, and Bible study to find a Bible-teaching church and begin to attend. We grow in our faith by connecting with mature believers who study and teach the Bible. The best friends of my life came from our church home. We share the same faith; we talk about our faith and grow together. We have laughed and cried through each of our joys and losses while praying for one another. These relationships would not have existed had we not responded to a postcard invitation.

The first time you walk into a church as a new believer, you may feel that all eyes are on you. You may think you will be rejected for how you have lived. Most of the time, this is not true. But if you are not comfortable there, go to another church that teaches the Bible.

The next step is to begin to study the Bible on your own. How can you understand what you are reading? Simply reading does not bring change from an old life to a new life. It is understanding and application of God's Word that changes lives. Once you commit your life to Jesus, you are sealed with the Holy Spirit of God within you. It is the Holy Spirit that gives you understanding.

> *In him you, also, when you heard the word of truth, the gospel of your salvation, and believed in him, were sealed with the promised Holy Spirit. (Ephesians 1:13)*

It is by God's Spirit that we are given wisdom and insight to understand. Therefore, as you begin to study, pray first asking God to grant you wisdom for understanding what you are reading.

There are many good methods for learning how to study the Bible. I like to say I cut my spiritual teeth on Precept Bible Studies by Kay Arthur. They are in-depth studies that not only teach the Bible, but how to *study* the Bible.

For believers in the culture of today, the study method taught by Katie Orr and Kathy Howard is great. With Katie's permission, I am sharing a blog post she wrote:

> *One of the most important things I did was attending my first Bible study class. I didn't know anything about the Bible but was in a class with seasoned believers. I didn't know how to find a specific book, chapter, or verse and was too embarrassed to look at the table of contents. But it is quicker to use the table of contents for a page number than to flip from cover to cover trying to locate the passage they are teaching fRomans You think all eyes are on you, but believe me, no one is condemning you for wanting to learn. In fact, they will help you. Use the table of contents.*

Four important actions to take to increase your faith and learn from God through his Word.

- Find a church home.
- Study the Bible.
- Learn to pray.
- Apply lessons for life.

Endnotes

1 Tozer, T. W., *The Pursuit of Man: The Divine Conquest of the Human Heart* (Camp Hill, PA: Wingspread Publishers, 2006).

2 Evans, Tony, *The Tony Evans Bible Commentary* (Nashville: Holman Bible Publishers, 2019).

3 Vine, W.E.; Unger, Merrill F.; White, Jr, William, *Vine's Complete Expository Dictionary of Old and New Testament Words* (Nashville: Thomas Nelson Publishers, 1985), 143.

4 Vine, et al., *Vine's Complete Expository Dictionary of Old and New Testament Words*, 122.

5 "Proclamation, Fasting, Humiliation, Prayer," *Wall Builders* (blog), April 20, 2023, wallbuilders.com/proclamation-fasting-humiliation-prayer-1789–connecticut/

Resources

Tandemprayer.org

Katieorr.me/Bible-study-hub

BlueletterBible.com

Kathyhoward.org

Logos Bible Software

Precept Ministries

VirginiaGrounds.net

BreakthroughChristianPublishing.com

About the Author

Virginia Grounds is an author, speaker, Bible study teacher, and podcaster. With decades of experience in women's ministry and teaching, her love of God's Word and sharing the gospel of Christ is evident. Her podcast, Quick Studies Podcast, continues teaching in a way that women who are busy can listen to a lesson each week right where they are. She has completed Biblical Studies from Liberty University. She also received an honorary Masters of Ministry to Women.

Virginia has written devotions as a guest blogger for Arise Daily, Beyond Ordinary Women, Majestic Inspirations, VirginiaGrounds.net (her own) and inkspirationsonline.com in addition to other books available on Amazon. She is a Certified Professional Publisher from NFAA, a speech coach, and P.O.W.E.R Speaker with Advanced Writers and Speakers Association.

- *Rock Solid Trust* – non-fiction – Nominated for the Christian Literary Award
- *Living Your Glory Story* – a Bible Study
- *Facing Fears, Quenching Flames* – a devotional
- *Ricky the Racecar* – a children's book

If You Enjoyed This Book, Will You Help Me Spread the Word?

There are several ways you can help me get the word out about the message of this book...

- Post a 5–Star review on Amazon.
- Write about the book on your Facebook, X, Instagram, LinkedIn, – any social media you regularly use!
- If you blog, consider referencing the book, or publishing an excerpt from the book with a link back to my website. You have my permission to do this if you provide proper credit and backlinks.
- Recommend the book to friends – word-of-mouth is still the most effective form of advertising.
- Purchase additional copies to give away as gifts.

The best way to connect is by visiting
VirginiaGrounds.net,
BreakthroughChristianPublishing.com,
or send an email to Virginia@VirginiaGrounds.net.